CAMBRIDGE LIBRARY COLLECTION

Books of enduring scholarly value

Egyptology

The large-scale scientific investigation of Egyptian antiquities by Western scholars began as an unintended consequence of Napoleon's invasion of Egypt during which, in 1799, the Rosetta Stone was discovered. The military expedition was accompanied by French scholars, whose reports prompted a wave of enthusiasm that swept across Europe and North America resulting in the Egyptian Revival style in art and architecture. Increasing numbers of tourists visited Egypt, eager to see the marvels being revealed by archaeological excavation. Writers and booksellers responded to this growing interest with publications ranging from technical site reports to tourist guidebooks and from children's histories to theories identifying the pyramids as repositories of esoteric knowledge. This series reissues a wide selection of such books. They reveal the gradual change from the 'tomb-robbing' approach of early excavators to the highly organised and systematic approach of Flinders Petrie, the 'father of Egyptology', and include early accounts of the decipherment of the hieroglyphic script.

The Revolutions of Civilisation

Among the leading Egyptologists of his day, Sir William Matthew Flinders Petrie (1853–1942) excavated over fifty sites and trained a generation of archaeologists. This short yet well-illustrated work, first published in 1911, sketches humankind's achievements over 10,000 years, establishing patterns in the rise and fall of civilisations. Drawing on his extensive knowledge of ancient Egypt, and looking also at Greece, Rome and beyond, Petrie defines each civilisation as having a summer of growth and a winter of decline, revealing his controversial eugenic view that while migration can initially reinvigorate a society, the mixing of peoples over time leads ultimately to that society's deterioration. Correlating developments in the production of art and material culture in different places, Petrie argues that civilisation is not a continuous state, but intermittent and recurrent. Many of his other publications – for both Egyptologists and non-specialists – are also reissued in this series.

T0364295

Cambridge University Press has long been a pioneer in the reissuing of out-of-print titles from its own backlist, producing digital reprints of books that are still sought after by scholars and students but could not be reprinted economically using traditional technology. The Cambridge Library Collection extends this activity to a wider range of books which are still of importance to researchers and professionals, either for the source material they contain, or as landmarks in the history of their academic discipline.

Drawing from the world-renowned collections in the Cambridge University Library and other partner libraries, and guided by the advice of experts in each subject area, Cambridge University Press is using state-of-the-art scanning machines in its own Printing House to capture the content of each book selected for inclusion. The files are processed to give a consistently clear, crisp image, and the books finished to the high quality standard for which the Press is recognised around the world. The latest print-on-demand technology ensures that the books will remain available indefinitely, and that orders for single or multiple copies can quickly be supplied.

The Cambridge Library Collection brings back to life books of enduring scholarly value (including out-of-copyright works originally issued by other publishers) across a wide range of disciplines in the humanities and social sciences and in science and technology.

The Revolutions
of Civilisation

W.M. FLINDERS PETRIE

CAMBRIDGE
UNIVERSITY PRESS

CAMBRIDGE
UNIVERSITY PRESS

University Printing House, Cambridge, CB2 8BS, United Kingdom

Published in the United States of America by Cambridge University Press, New York

Cambridge University Press is part of the University of Cambridge.
It furthers the University's mission by disseminating knowledge in the pursuit of
education, learning and research at the highest international levels of excellence.

www.cambridge.org
Information on this title: www.cambridge.org/9781108065818

© in this compilation Cambridge University Press 2013

This edition first published 1911
This digitally printed version 2013

ISBN 978-1-108-06581-8 Paperback

HARPER'S LIBRARY *of* LIVING THOUGHT

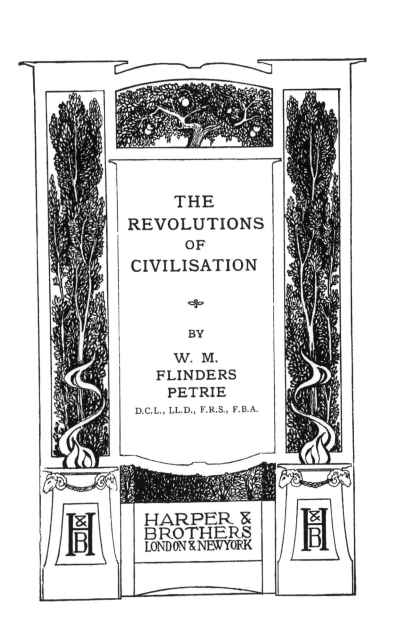

THE
REVOLUTIONS
OF
CIVILISATION

BY

W. M.
FLINDERS
PETRIE
D.C.L., LL.D., F.R.S., F.B.A.

HARPER &
BROTHERS
LONDON & NEW YORK

THE REVOLUTIONS
OF CIVILISATION

BY

W. M. FLINDERS PETRIE

D.C.L., LL.D., F.R.S., F.B.A.

AUTHOR OF
"PERSONAL RELIGION IN EGYPT BEFORE CHRISTIANITY"
"EGYPT AND ISRAEL" "ARTS AND CRAFTS OF
ANCIENT EGYPT"
ETC.

LONDON AND NEW YORK

HARPER & BROTHERS

45 ALBEMARLE STREET, W.

1911

Published April, 1911

CONTENTS

CONTENTS

LIST OF ILLUSTRATIONS

LIST OF ILLUSTRATIONS

x ii

THE REVOLUTIONS OF
CIVILISATION

CHAPTER I

THE NATURE OF CIVILISATION

(1) THE MEANING OF LIFE

THE meaning of Life has in all ages been
the goal of human thought. The search
for the causes and effects of the changes that
man has undergone has laid the foundations of
his religion and his philosophy. The solutions
of the different problems have been as inaccu-
rate as they are varied ; nor could any better
results be expected from the very insufficient
acquaintance with the past.

The last fifty years have greatly extended
our knowledge of history, and we stand on a
very different footing to all those who in earlier
times have dealt with the position of man.
While, formerly, nothing could be learned that
was not in written record, handed down from
generation to generation, we now handle manu-

scripts that last saw the light when Rome ruled, we read the records that were compiled thousands of years before the Father of History, and we know how to reconstruct the unwritten past from the many other activities and products of human work.

It seems, therefore, that the time has arrived when we may begin to take some general outlook over the history of human nature. Our material for observation is far greater than others have had. Our method is more developed since we have learned that comparison is the principal—or almost the only—useful line of study. Can we then extract a meaning from all the ceaseless turmoil and striving, and success and failure, of these thousands of years ? Can we see any regular structure behind it all ? Can we learn any general principles that may formulate the past, or be projected on the mists of the future ?

Hitherto the comparatively brief outlook of Western history has given us only the great age of classical civilisation before modern times. We have been in the position of a child that remembers only a single summer before that which he enjoys. To such an one the cold, dark, miserable winter that has intervened seems a needless and inexplicable interruption of a happier order—of a summer which should never cease. Only a few years ago a writer of

2

1. THE GRAVE STELE OF HEGESO. ATHENS.

THE NATURE OF CIVILISATION

repute deplored the mysterious fall of the Roman Empire, which in his view ought to have been always prosperous, and never have fallen to the barbarians. He was the child who could not understand the winter.

(2) INTERMITTENT CIVILISATION

From what we now know, it is evident, even on the most superficial view, that civilisation is an intermittent phenomenon. When we look at Greek art—as in the exquisite grave steles (fig. 1) ; then at the decay, before the time of the barbarian invasions—as in the figure of Bellicia (Felicia) from the catacombs (fig. 2) ; and then, again, at the splendid sculpture of the fifteenth century—as in the San Giorgio of Donatello (fig. 3), the intermission of art is obvious. We therefore need to compare the various periods, to see what they have in common, and to gather what may be taken as the type of them all.

Further, when on a longer view we can trace in the East several intermissions, we may say that civilisation is a recurrent phenomenon. As such it should be examined like any other action of Nature ; its recurrences should be studied, and all the principles which underlie its variations should be defined.

(3) Sculpture the Definite Test

We need to look at some one feature of the complex mass of interests which are grouped under the name of civilisation, in order to make accurate comparisons. We should only be con-

2. The Grave Stele of Bellicia. Rome.

3. San Giorgio, by Donatello. Florence.

fused if we contrast things differing in their nature, such as Egyptian construction, Greek poetry, and mediaeval self-denial. Though sculpture is only one, and not the most important, of the many subjects that might be compared throughout various ages, yet it is available over so long a period, in so many countries, and so readily presented to the mind, that it may be well to begin with that as a standard subject for comparison, and afterwards look at other activities.

(4) THE GREAT YEAR

We have used the simile of summer and winter for the growth and fall of civilisation. This analogy of the Great Year was familiar to the ancients ; in the East, Berossos, the Babylonian, writes of the summer and winter of the Great Year ; in the West, the Etruscans also spoke of the Great Year as the period of each race of men that should arise in succession. When their own Great Year, of 1100 years, came to an end in the turbulent time of Sulla (87 B.C.), we read : " One day when the sky was serene and clear there was heard in it the sound of a trumpet, so shrill and mournful that it frightened and astonished the whole city. The Tuscan sages said that it portended a new race of men, and a renovation of the

9

world, for they observed that there were eight
several kinds of men, all differing in life and
manners ; that heaven had allotted to each its
time, which was limited by the circuit of the
Great Year ; and that when one race came to
a period, and another was rising, it was an-
nounced by some wonderful sign from either
earth or heaven. So that it was evident at one
view to those who attended to these things, and
were versed in them, that a different sort of
men was come into the world, with other manners and customs, and more or less the care of
the gods than those who had preceded them.
. . . Such was the mythology of the most
learned and respectable of the Tuscan sooth-
sayers " (Plutarch, in *Sulla*). Apart from the
innate belief in divination, we see the broad
idea which the Etruscans had of history, that
each successive race had its period of a Great
Year in which it sprouted, flourished, decayed,
and died. And the simile is the more precise,
as there may be bright warm days in winter,
or cold times in summer, and there are always
irregular fluctuations of weather. So in the
course of each civilisation there are similar
variations, but they do not prevent our recog-
nising the broad outlines of its summer and its
winter.

CHAPTER II

THE PERIODS OF CIVILISATION

TO learn what the nature of any recurring phenomenon may be, we should examine the longest series of its revolutions and see what they have in common. In Egypt we can trace the past of man in continuous history for over seven thousand years, and can put in order a prehistoric age which may well extend our view to about ten thousand years. Over the whole of that time we know what were the products of every century. In that long range of vision we can discern eight successive periods of civilisation, each separated by an age of barbarism or decline before and after it. Here, then, the discoveries of the last twenty years have put in our hands a series which is sufficient to enable us to compare periods together, and learn what they may have in common. We shall here denote these periods by Roman numerals I to VIII ; and the stages in other countries which may be contemporary will bear the same numbers.

(5) THE IST PERIOD : PREHISTORIC

Apart from the palaeolithic flint age, which cannot be treated consecutively, the beginning of the continuous civilisation of Egypt is seen in the shallow circular pits which each contain a body doubled up, with a goat's skin thrown over it, and a simple pot and saucer at its side. Shortly after this stage a variety of pottery appears, all of the same materials, among which are red cups and vases decorated with white cross lines, like the modern Algerian ware. This painted pottery gives us the best material for observing the changes of the age, as it is fairly abundant, and has been already classified into several stages by its relations to other kinds of pottery. We see in the earlier examples of this pottery (fig. 4) the careful imitation of basket-work lines, with the central circle on which the basket was built. In the middle stage the circle is dropped ; the decoration has almost freed itself from the basket origin, and has become a clear and independent design, a Maltese cross with sprigs between the arms. In the late stage only an unintelligent degradation of the basket pattern has survived. Thus, in this most remote age, there is proof of the rise of ornament from natural imitation, the development of it as pure ornament, and its decay in unintelligent copying. The few remains from this age of any artistic bearing do not suffice to trace a regular sequence like this in other materials. But the general style of the pottery was rising in character and variety for some time, and the work in hard stones and flint was largely developed. The connections of this age are with the West, in the style and decoration of the pottery.

EGYPT. Ist PERIOD.

EARLY   MIDDLE   LATE

4. GROWTH AND DECAY OF PATTERNS ON WHITE SLIP BOWLS.

(6) THE IIND PERIOD: PREHISTORIC

A new order arises with various eastern connections. Almost every kind of product was changed. The older pottery ceased to develop new types, and only lingered on in decay; by its side a coarser style appears with entirely new decoration in red. Stone vases changed from tubular to barrel shapes. The forms of flints, of slate palettes, of ivory working, and the material of beads, all start afresh. The burials are all single, instead of two or more together, as in earlier times. Throughout this later time a continuous decay may be seen (fig. 5), which we can illustrate by the forms of slate palettes, degrading from the tortoise or fish to a senseless outline, and the rise and decay of flint working, which was the special art of this age. The degradation of all the products down to the close of the period is very marked, not only in those here illustrated, but also in the abundant pottery, which became coarse and rough, without any artistic feeling.

(7) THE IIIRD PERIOD : O–IIND DYNASTIES

The distinctive art of Egypt begins to appear shortly before the Ist dynasty. Hieroglyphic writing was being rapidly developed from an ideographic stage, and we see the rise of a bold, naturalistic style of sculpture. The archaic stage is seen in the vigorous figure of a warrior (fig. 6), carrying his standard and flourishing his double-headed axe. By the time of Mena, who founded the Ist dynasty, the carving was emerging from the archaic, though not yet free.

THE PERIODS OF CIVILISATION

The head of a king in limestone (fig. 7) is of this age, or slightly later. By the second dynasty decay had set in, and the bad proportions and

EGYPT. IIND PERIOD.

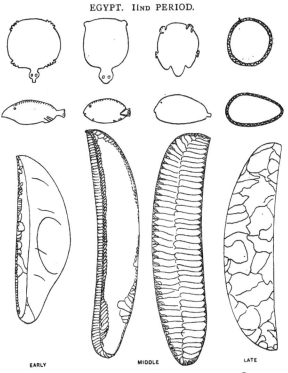

EARLY MIDDLE LATE

5. GROWTH AND DECAY OF FLINTWORK AND SLATE ANIMAL FIGURES.

pose of the red granite figure (fig. 8) are quite
out of keeping with the work of the previous
dynasty. For a more consecutive view of the
changes we may look at the series of royal
hawks (fig. 9), emblems of the king's soul.
They are enlarged here, and therefore detail is
not to be looked for. The eight at the beginning are of the eight kings of the Ist dynasty,
the other four are of the IInd and IIIrd dynasties. The first figure—of the time of Mena—
hardly attempts the characteristics of a hawk.
In the second figure the form of the wings and
the shape of the head have been seized. In the
third figure the type is at its best ; the points
of the bird are fully grasped, as in the detail
of the marking near the eye and on the neck,
the feathering of the legs, and the gripping
claws. The fourth observes these points, but
in the artificial style of a copyist. The fifth
and sixth rapidly deteriorate ; and further on
there are only fluctuations of decay, the later
ones even losing the form of the head, and copying the type as mere routine. These hawks
serve as an example of the rapid rise, the current
changes, and the long decay of art, in the
first three dynasties. The degree of correct-
ness of these drawings corresponds very closely,
reign by reign, with the work of the royal
tombs of the kings and the general products.
The third figure comes from the largest and

7. STUDY IN LIMESTONE OF EARLY KING.
BEST PERIOD.

6. PREHISTORIC WARRIOR.
SLATE PALETTE.
ARCHAIC.

8. GRANITE FIGURE.
DECADENT. IIND DYN.

C

EGYPT.   IIIrd PERIOD.

NARMER   AHA   ZER

ZET   DEN   AZAB

SEMERKHET   QA   HOTEPAHAUI

PERABSEN   KHASEKHEMUI   NETER-KHET

9.   GROWTH AND DECAY OF HAWK FIGURES.

finest tomb ; the sixth is from the worst tomb, even inferior to those that follow. The best hardstone vases are of the middle of the dynasty, the softer stones are commoner at the close of the dynasty, while stone vases are much scarcer in the IInd dynasty, and in the IIIrd only soft alabaster is found. In every respect, therefore, the beginning of the Ist dynasty is archaic, the early middle is the finest age, and from that onwards there is only a little fluctuation in the decay. The sculpture of the early third dynasty in Sinai is the rudest there, and is unspeakably worse than the excellent figures from the first dynasty.

(8) THE IVTH PERIOD : IIIRD–VITH DYNASTIES

There now arises the great age of the Pyramid Builders, at the close of the IIIrd dynasty. The rise of the art was probably as rapid as in the Ist dynasty. There is an interval of only 130 years in the lists between the king whose work is the worst (Neterkhet) and the almost perfect art of Sneferu. Unfortunately we have no examples definitely dated to the rise of this art, but we can see the remains of its archaic period in the portrait of Queen Mertitefs (fig. 10). The careful working of detail separately, without treating it as part of a whole to be blended together, is the essential mark of archaism. The well-known head of Nefert (fig. 11) must, again, appear as the earliest figure of the pyramid age which is perfectly free in execution. An example of the relief sculpture is shown in the vigorous design of the boatmen (fig. 12). In contrast to this, we see how low this art sank in the early part of the XIth dynasty by the figure of Antefa (fig. 13). Every stage of gradual decay can be traced through the intervening age.

These changes in the art agree with the state of the architecture. It rose to its greatest accuracy of work, and boldest handling of immense masses, in the generation which saw the statue of Nefert; and from that point there was continuous decline. The buildings were less in size and inferior in work, until in the VIth dynasty the masses of the pyramids were merely of loose rubble. In the rest of this period no pyramids are known, the small brick ones in the XIth dynasty rather belonging to the rise of the next period. As Mr. Griffith has remarked, " The art of engraving monumental inscriptions had deteriorated greatly as early as the VIth dynasty all over Egypt, even in the centres of civilisation ; . . . from the VIth to the XIth dynasty the barbaric stelae present many extraordinary attempts to render the half-forgotten signs in detail. With the monu-

10. QUEEN MERTITEFS. CAIRO.

11. PRINCESS NEFERT. CAIRO.

12. FIGHT OF BOATMEN. VTH DYN. CAIRO.

13. ANTEFA. XITH DYN. DENDEREH.

mental revival at the end of the XIth dynasty the knowledge of hieroglyphs revived " (Petrie, *Dendereh*, 53).

(9) THE VTH PERIOD :
VIITH–XIVTH DYNASTIES

This period opens with a minute attention to detail, much like the archaism of the pre-Persian sculptures in Greece. The varieties of growth can be best seen in the sculptures from Dendereh, and a well-advanced example is the tablet at Marseille (fig. 14). The rise of this new art was rapid up to its full beauty in the XIIth dynasty. The XIth dynasty may have occupied, at most, two centuries from its first princedom, and the old style lasted well into its early stages. Probably the whole rise occupied only a century, and certainly not more than a century and a half.

Under Amenemhat I, the most delicate low relief was in use, as in the head of Min shown here (fig. 15). The hard modelling and bad proportion of the XIth dynasty head has developed rapidly into the most refined relief.

By the latter part of the XIIth dynasty there was a manifest decline, as for instance in the head of Amenemhat III here given (fig. 16). The continuous series of scarabs shows the same decline ; finest and most perfect under Senusert I, they steadily became coarsened down to the end of the dynasty, and those of the XIIIth and XIVth dynasties show a continued decadence. The best sculpture of the XIIIth dynasty kept up some of the earlier style, but was weak and formal, as in the figure of Neferhotep (fig. 17). The later stages of this period are lost in the darkness of civil confusion and decay, finally closed by the Hyksos invasion.

(10) THE VITH PERIOD :
XVTH–XXTH DYNASTIES

This age is the best known, owing to the profusion of remains, especially at Thebes. Of the archaic stage one of the most vigorous examples is the scene of dancers (fig. 18), which resembles the coffin paintings of the XVIIth dynasty. In the XVIIIth dynasty there were several stages with different styles. At first a delicate and ingenuous type prevailed, especially on the statuettes, as in the head here shown (fig. 19). The foreign conquests, which brought in Syrian influence, changed the type. The best example of its portraiture is that of Tahutmes III (fig. 20) ; and after his time greater richness of material and variety of colour was reached, but with a less decided style. The great break of the naturalism of

14. HEAD OF HOTEPTU. MARSEILLE.

15. HEAD OF MIN. UNIV. COLL., LONDON.

16. AMENEMHAT III. CAIRO.

17. NEFERHOTEP III. BOLOGNA.

31

18. FRESCO OF DANCERS. XVIITH DYN. OXFORD.

19. HEAD OF STATUETTE. TURIN.
SEE ARCHAIC, VIITH PERIOD, FIG. 39.

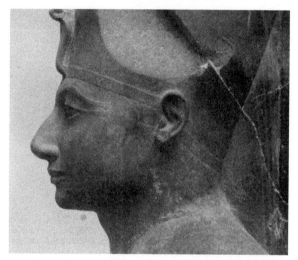

20. TAHUTMES III. BASALT. CAIRO.

21. RAMESSU II. RED GRANITE LUQSOR

Akhenaten, and the revulsion from it, closed the dynasty. After that there was only continuous decay, as seen in the later sculpture of Ramessu II (fig. 21).

(11) THE VIITH PERIOD:
XXIST–XXXIIIRD DYNASTIES

The scarcity of statuary prevents our seeing the lowest stage of the new period. The statue of Amenardys (fig. 22) has, however, some heaviness and lack of proportion, which afterwards disappears. The XXVIth dynasty excelled in portraiture, such as the basalt head here shown (fig. 23). Its reliefs, though without the real vitality of the Old Kingdom which supplied the model, yet show considerable grace and ingenious design, as in the row of bearers carrying farm produce (fig. 24). The depth to which this art sank may be guessed from the head of a Roman statue (fig. 25), which is by no means the worst of its kind. Greek and Roman art was too incongruous to be a prop to Egyptian design, and the old style passed away for ever.

(12) THE VIIITH PERIOD : THE ARAB

How base the style became is painfully seen in the Coptic sculpture (fig. 26). The influences upon it were the decayed classical, and the

Persian art; and it is curious how the geometrical style of the Arab art is anticipated
in the straight lines and mechanical curves of
the Coptic figures.

The Muslim, abandoning all animate forms,
cannot be judged in the same manner as the
workers of earlier periods. We must turn to
his architecture for comparisons of style. The
early work, as in the Citadel and fortifications
of Cairo, might almost pass as one with the
Norman, which was contemporary with it in
Europe. The gate Bab-el-Futuh shown here
(fig. 27) was built in 1087, the period of the
Tower of London and Malling Abbey; for
other comparisons see Chapter IV. The squares
of pattern on the arch follow in pairs on oppo-
site sides, but without any repetitions in either
side, just as in the pairs of mosaic bands along
the walls of the Cathedral at Monreale. Note
the grand relieving arch, high above the gate-
way arch. Coming down to the full-blown
period of the XIVth century, that of the
Decorated style in England, we see (fig. 28)
in the porch of the entrance of Sultan Hasan's
mosque (1358), the development of elaborate
bracketing around the recess, to contract the
span sufficiently to throw a safe arch over it.
The relieving arch has shrunk to a useless band
of masonry. Next, the decay of this design
is shown (fig. 29) in the gate of Kait Bey (1480),

22. HEAD OF AMENARDYS. CAIRO.

23. BASALT HEAD. LOUVRE

24. YOUTH AND MAIDS WITH OFFERINGS. CAIRO.

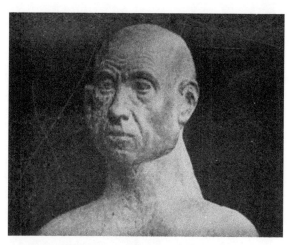

25. ROMAN STATUE. BERLIN.

41

26. EARLY COPTIC HEAD. UNIV. COLL., LONDON.

27. BAB-EL-FUTUH. A.D. 1087. CAIRO.

28. Porch of Sultan Hasan. a.d. 1358. Cairo.

29. Porch of Kait Bey. a.d. 1480. Cairo.

equivalent to the Perpendicular style, where the noble deep recess is flattened out to a surface decoration, the bracketing has changed to mere superficial pendentives, and the decadence is evident.

We have now seen how we can trace through eight successive periods the repeated growth, glory, and decay of art in Egypt, indicating the revolutions of civilisation through some ten thousand years.

CHAPTER III

THE PERIODS OF CIVILISATION IN EUROPE

(13) The IVth Period : The Early Cretan Age

THIS period was contemporary with the IVth period of Egypt, and is the earliest that has yet been clearly disentangled in Europe. The remains parallel to the first three periods in Egypt still lie in the 21 feet of neolithic ruins at Knossos ; this depth is a greater amount of accumulation than that which contained the ruins of the subsequent three periods of the Early, Middle, and Late Cretan Ages. I have to thank Dr. Evans for assigning the relative periods of many Cretan remains which do not appear in his printed *Classification*, and for supplying several illustrations.

Of the Early Cretan Age the most important examples have not yet been published, those found at Mochlos. It is hardly practicable to show the growth and decay of art clearly from the published material ; and we therefore only give here the remains from the tholos tomb at

30. OBJECTS FROM THOLOS OF HAGIA TRIADA.

31. Polychrome Vase. Knossos.

32. Faience, Goat and Kids. Knossos.

Hagia Triada. The seals (fig. 30) are primitive in style ; the two dogs with leaf pattern are the best work here ; the wavy band is apparently the earliest stage of the spiral patterns, which dominated the art of Europe in later periods. There is also an elaborate wavy band pattern on a square plaque. The figures are like those of the Egyptian prehistoric age, period II, having no arms, and the legs ending in a point. They show the earliest rise of figure-carving. The well-known Greek " island figures " from the Cyclades belong to this age.

(14) THE VTH PERIOD : THE MIDDLE
CRETAN AGE

In the Vth period the main feature is the development of brilliant polychrome painting on the vases, and the broad designs of noble curves (fig. 31). The period begins with rude figures of men and fishes, and the founding of the first palace at Knossos. There is a steady growth of naturalism ; and at the close of this period there is the shrine of Knossos, with the goddess holding snakes. There is also the beautiful group of the goat and kids (fig. 32) ; both of these examples are wrought in coloured glazed ware. A general catastrophe ended this period.

REVOLUTIONS OF CIVILISATION

(15) The VIth Period : The Late Cretan Age

We here reach the period of art which is the rival, if not the superior, of the classical age. The level from which it sprang is seen in the fisherman of Phylakopi (fig. 33) ; there, though the drawing is crude, the sense of action and vitality of it is full of promise. The splendid steatite vases with reliefs of figures soon follow on this. How the figure-painting developed is seen by the magnificent figure of the vase-bearer (fig. 34), and the other spirited frescoes of that time. The masterpieces of the gold cups of Vapheio, with the scenes of bulls (fig. 35), show the greatest amount of spirit. The bronze vases have beautiful leaf patterns embossed around them. The pottery vases have paintings of tall lilies, life-size, which remind us of the finest Florentine work. The architecture was grand and elaborate, as seen in the great palace of Knossos.

But all this splendour suffered a sudden catastrophe in the Dorian invasion ; the remains of the style lingered on in some places, as seen in the grave slab from Mykenae (fig. 36), and the Cypriote vase-painting of a chariot (fig. 37). Those centres which were not occupied by the Dorians, as Cyprus, and some cities on the mainland such as Athens, retained the decayed forms of their old arts.

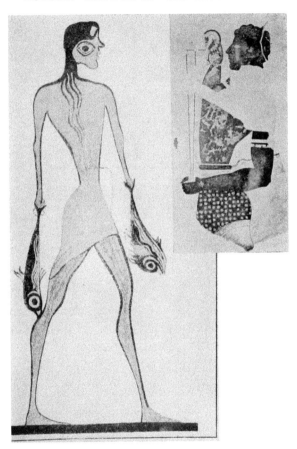

33. FISHERMAN. PHYLAKOPI. 34. VASE BEARER. KNOSSOS.

35. BULLS ON GOLD CUP. VAPHEIO.

36. GRAVE STELE. MYKENAE.

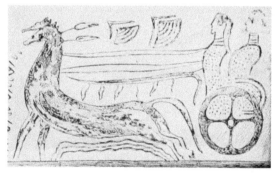

37. CHARIOT ON VASE. CYPRUS.

CIVILISATION IN EUROPE

(16) The VIIth Period : Classical

The rise of a new art began to dawn in the dipylon vases. The rich spirals of the older art give way to fret patterns ; and geometrical rectilinear decoration and motives take the place of the free design of forms in action. Fresh styles of architecture arise, and Asiatic influences supply the new motives. The figures are stiff and formal, as in the head, probably of Athena, who appears inciting Perseus to the decapitation of Medusa ; this metope of Selinus (fig. 38) is of the early part of the VIth century B.C. A century later the sculpture had advanced to its most expressive stage, and almost its highest technical perfection, as in the statues of maidens on the Acropolis at Athens (fig. 39). To this succeeded the perfect freedom of work in the figure of the piping maiden (fig. 40) upon the end of the Ludovisi throne, and the stele of Hegeso (fig. 1). The great mass of Greek sculpture gradually fell off from this standard during several centuries. Then next come the still lower Roman copies of Greek work, of wearying banality, until we reach the stumpy, clumsy figures of the age of Constantine (fig. 41), or the still coarser outlines from the catacomb tombs, such as that of Bellicia (fig. 2).

(17) The VIIIth Period : Mediaeval

The Northern immigrants brought new ideals with them into the Mediterranean world ; and an entirely different style arose, which in its vertical lines and lengthy figures recalls the pre-classical work of Italy, and the attenuated style of Celtic animals. An example of an early stage (A.D. 1139) is the scene of an exorcism, embossed in bronze, on the gate of San Zeno at Verona (fig. 42). The bishop and a monk are holding the arms of the possessed woman, from whose mouth a devil is jumping out. This is the parallel, in this period, to the Selinus designs in the previous period.

A century later the nearly perfect work is reached of the Ecclesia at Bamberg (fig. 43), which should be compared to the similar stage in period VII shown in fig. 39. The last trace of archaism in this overlaps the age of the most perfect sculpture, as seen in the head of the Emperor Henry VI at Bamberg (fig. 44), about 1245 A.D.

How much Europe afterwards deteriorated is painfully seen in all the later sculpture, until in Elizabethan or Jacobean times we reach such productions as the alabaster effigy of Robert Dudley at Warwick (fig. 45).

Nor was this decline peculiar to these examples. Compare the figures of the English

38. HEAD OF ATHENA, SELINUS. PALERMO.

39. HEAD OF MAIDEN. ATHENS.

40. PIPING MAIDEN, LUDOVISI THRONE.

41. TRIUMPH OF CONSTANTINE. ROME.

42. SCENE OF EXORCISM. S. ZENO, VERONA.

F

43. ECCLESIA. A.D. 1245. BAMBERG.
COMPARE VII ARCHAIC, FIG. 39,
AND VI ARCHAIC, FIG. 19.

*Photo: Dr. Fr. Stoedtner,
Berlin, N.W.*

67

44. KAISER HEINRICH VI. A.D. 1245. BAMBERG.

Photo: Dr. Fr. Stoedtner,
Berlin, N.W.

45. ROBERT DUDLEY. WARWICK.

queens. That of Eleanor (fig. 46), queen of Henry II, at Fontevrault, with its archaic smile and arrangement of drapery, dates about 1190. By 1290 there is the exquisitely graceful figure of Eleanor of Castile at Westminster (fig. 47). The statue of Anne of Bohemia has retained the grace of expression, but the dress has become stiffer by 1395, while Joan of Navarre (fig. 48) shows much more formalism in 1415.

In the series of brasses the same decline is very familiar, though the series does not begin early enough to show the archaic stage. Perhaps the most perfect in design is that of Joan de Cobham in 1320 (fig. 49), and for the grace of attitude and flow of the drapery this is unsurpassed. Descending a century, we meet the stiff lines, bad anatomy of the arms, and formal expression of Lady Bagot in 1407 (fig. 50).

Yet another century later, in 1512, the style has become entirely stiff and wooden, as in the brass of Anne Astley (fig. 51), with the swaddled twins in her arms. And in another century, by 1605, we have passed out of all the traditions, and reach an age of trivial externals in the figure of Aphra Hawkins (fig. 52).

The same degradation appears on the seals of the kings and others. Perhaps the most perfect artistic feeling on any seal is seen in that of Simon de Montfort, with the hunter at full gallop, blowing his horn, engraved about 1240. By the fifteenth century the designs of the great seals had become heavy, formal, and badly proportioned.

Thus we see, in every branch of sculpture and engraving, how the latter part of the thirteenth century was the turning point when complete mastery was attained, and how continual was the decay after that time. The Renascence was but the resort of copying an earlier period, owing to the decay and loss of the true style of the VIIIth, or Mediaeval, age of Art. The history of copying—good, bad, or indifferent—does not concern us here ; copying is an artificial system, which has no natural development or root in the mind, and which browses indifferently on anything that may be the fashion of the day.

46. ELEANOR
QUEEN OF
HENRY II.
FONTEVRAULT.
1190.

47. ELEANOR
OF CASTILE.
EDWARD I.
WESTMINSTER.
1290.

48. JOAN
OF NAVARRE.
HENRY IV.
WESTMINSTER.
1415.

49. JOAN DE COBHAM.
1320.

50. LADY BAGOT
1407.

51. ANNE ASTLEY.
1512.

52. APHRA HAWKINS.
1605.

CHAPTER IV

THE FLUCTUATIONS

(18) Egypt and Europe Contemporary

THE many recurrences of civilisation in Egypt and in Europe which we have observed, suggest the question as to how far these changes are contemporary—that is to say, in the same phase at one time.

To take the most recent age, we may compare some of the best-known buildings of the VIIIth period.

East.	England.
The massive fortifications.	
Cairo Gates, 1087–1091.	Tower of London, 1078.
	Newcastle, 1080.
The beginning of lighter style.	
Cairo Citadel, 1183.	Canterbury choir, 1180.
Dome of the Rock, 1189.	Lincoln choir, 1186.
End of good enrichment.	
Mosque of Sultan Hasan,	Trinity College,
Cairo, 1362.	Cambridge, 1350.
	Gloucester choir, 1350.
Overloaded decoration, pendentives.	
Tomb of Kait Bey, 1474.	Crosby Hall, 1470.
Palace of Yeshbek, 1476.	St. George's, Windsor, 1476.

It will be seen that, even as far apart as Egypt and England, right across Europe, the developments of the two architectures were as nearly contemporary as we can estimate them. There was certainly not a century of discrepancy.

In the VIIth period it is difficult to date the Egyptian position ; for there are very few dated sculptures after 1000 B.C. until we reach Ptolemaic times, when Greek influence prevailed. The new style was beginning by 600 B.C., was strong by 550, and had fully developed by 525 at the Persian invasion. On the Greek side the architecture was strong before 600 B.C. (Corinth, Selinus), and fully developed by 500 (Agrigentum), though sculpture did not well develop till 500, or lose its archaism till 450 B.C. In this period, therefore, the Egyptian phase was half a century or a century before the Greek phase, doubtless due to the much larger amount of older models known to the Egyptian.

In the VIth period the archaism disappears in Egypt about 1550 B.C. ; a free style is reached by 1500, and decadence is clear by 1300. At Knossos the highest point of this period is at the close of the second palace, which by its Egyptian connections was about 1500 B.C. ; and the Tell-el-Amarna pottery of 1370 B.C. belongs to the decadence in Crete. Here we may say that there is not a century of discrepancy in the phase of the two countries.

The Vth period in Crete has its middle stage

linked with the middle of the XIIth dynasty in Egypt, and from the time of its decadence there comes a statuette of the XIIIth dynasty. The phase was therefore the same within two or three centuries ; but the material does not define the connection closer than that.

For the IVth period the later stage of it in Crete is linked, by the seal patterns, with the VIth–VIIIth dynasties in Egypt. And the IIIrd period in Egypt has pottery which seems to have been imported from Crete, where it is found in the " sub-neolithic," or stratum immediately on the neolithic level, and before any palace buildings. The Ist and IInd periods of Egypt are yet to be sought in the 25 feet of ruins of the neolithic age at Knossos, or 15 feet at Phaistos.

Thus it seems that the phase of the wave of civilisation was identical in Egypt and Europe to within a century, where it can be observed in three periods ; and that in three earlier periods it was generally connected, and may have been identical. The Mediterranean and Egypt, as a whole, form therefore a single group in the history of civilisation.

(19) LENGTH OF PERIOD

The length of period thus shown by the sculpture is next to be considered. Here the question of early chronology comes in, which has been fully discussed this year in " Historical Studies " (British School in Egypt) ; I shall therefore take it as there stated.   No valid reason has yet been given for abandoning the history written by the Egyptians, which is strongly supported by external evidence at each stage, and was accepted by all the older Egyptologists.

The best-defined position in the development of art is the close of the archaic age in sculpture, when a perfect harmonising of the several parts is first reached.   This is independent of personal taste, which may prefer this stage, or the archaic rather before it, or the full-blown glory rather later.   We may take the close of the archaic at the following dates :—

	INTERVAL.
VIIIth period, A.D. 1240	
	—1690
VIIth period, B.C. 450	
	—1100
VIth period, B.C. 1550	
	—1900
Vth period, B.C. 3450	
	—1300
IVth period, B.C. 4750	
	—650
IIIrd period, B.C. 5400	

THE FLUCTUATIONS

Thus the average period is 1330 years : the shortest about half that amount, and the longest about half as long again.

(20) CURVES OF EGYPTIAN AND EUROPEAN ART

We can now give some appreciation of the waves of art in the successive periods (fig. 53).

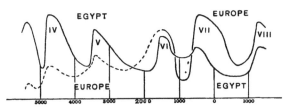

53. WAVES OF ART, IN EGYPT AND EUROPE.

It is, of course, a more or less personal matter how far certain periods are to be ranked on the same, or on a different, level. But the judgment of it is very constant, as my estimate made eleven years ago, and not referred to since, is almost identical in height of curves and in form of rise and fall, except in one or two details, where later discoveries have added to our knowledge, and in the addition of the waves III to V on the European side, which were then quite unknown.

The upper curve at the beginning shows the fluctuations in Egyptian art. The IIIrd period

(Ist dynasty) is intermediate in quality between the IVth and Vth periods (IVth and XIIth dynasties). Its art is as good as the IVth period, and much better than the Vth ; but its architecture is inferior to either. The VIth period (XVIIIth dynasty) is rather inferior in every way to the Vth. The decadence from it scarcely rises up to the VIIth period, the whole excellence of which is derived from copying. The VIIIth period (Arab), which has no sculpture in Egypt, it is impossible to assess, except by the general artistic products of architecture and metal work. Judged by these, it may fairly be put as equal to the VIIth (Saite) period.

There is another way also to compare these periods. The crest of one wave is on the same level as part of the decline of another wave ; and the art of the two points should be equivalent. For instance, the highest of the Vth period (XIIth dynasty) is equal to 800 years down the IVth period (or the middle of the Vth dynasty), and this seems fair. Similarly, the highest of period III is equal to 300 years down period IV (or the beginning of the Vth dynasty). Period VI (XVIIIth dynasty) is ranged as equal to 150 years down period V (or the middle of the XIIth dynasty). Similarly, the Saite period (VIIth) is reckoned equal to that of Rameses II. This may be a low estimate of

THE FLUCTUATIONS

it, but as all the good work at that date is only copying, we could hardly rank it higher.

The lower curve at the beginning is that of European art, which rises to be the higher at the end. As all architecture and sculpture since 1500 has been mere copying and playing variations, without any continuous natural development, the last four centuries are omitted as being very variously appreciated. For my own part, I should regard this VIIIth period as declining like the others, without taking into account an entirely artificial archaistic revival of the last fifty years, which has no root in the feelings of the majority, and will die like all mere fashions. No doubt in Hadrian's time they worshipped archaistic Minervas as the revival of beauty. All this, however, is only a personal opinion which I do not care to defend.

The mediaeval wave (VIII) is here ranked as intermediate in value between the Mykenaean (VI) and the Classical (VII). Such heads as Henry the Lion at Brunswick (A.D. 1227), and the Emperor Henry at Bamberg (1240), are more perfect expressions of character, free of conventionality, than anything which the Mykenaean age can show. They are fairly equal to the best portraiture of the 1st century B.C.; and accordingly the crest of the mediaeval wave (VIII) is put as equivalent to 50 B.C. The Mykenaean wave (VI) is put at the level of the

Antonines ; it is impossible to·equate work so much differing in feeling, but we could scarcely say that it was equal to either earlier or later work.

The depth of degradation of the chariot on the Cypriote vase (fig. 37) is certainly below anything in the eighth century A.D. By 600 B.C. there was a considerable rise, as in the Selinus metopes ; by 550 almost perfect work was reached, and it is hard to choose between 500 and 450 for the best. The fall of classical work was uniformly continuous from about 400 B.C. to A.D. 200. At each century the work was distinctly poorer than that of a hundred years before it. The rapid descent comes later, after Commodus or Severus, as best seen on the coinage. And the coinage also shows how A.D. 600–800 was the bottom of all in art. In the rise of mediaeval art, Henry I (1135 at Rochester) is below Mykenaean art ; Henry II, at Fontevrault (1190), is a great advance, showing only a little archaism ; and by 1240 the crest is reached. Such are the grounds for judging the form of the waves of the best-known ages of Europe. That the mediaeval was but little below the classical level may be seen not only in the heads of figs. 43, 44, but also in the technical work of drapery, where we may compare the finest Greek example, the Nikē (fig. 54) with the advancing work of fig. 55,

EUROPE. TECHNICAL SCULPTURE, VIITH AND VIIITH PERIODS.

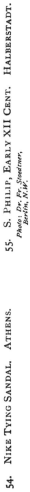

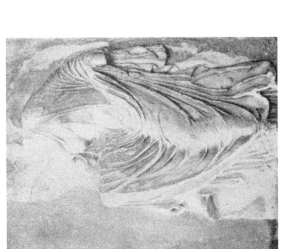

54. NIKE TYING SANDAL. ATHENS.

55. S. PHILIP, EARLY XII CENT. HALBERSTADT.

Photo: Dr. Fr. Stoedtner,
Berlin, N.W.

EUROPE. TECHNICAL SCULPTURE, VIIITH PERIOD.

56. DEATH OF THE VIRGIN. MID. XIII CENT. STRASSBURG.

THE FLUCTUATIONS

and the fully wrought figures of the death of the Virgin (fig. 56); these examples form an instructive comparison of the treatment of thin and thick draperies.

The earlier periods III, IV, V in Europe are only sketched in the diagram; their values are scarcely comparable with others, since there is no figure sculpture, and the vase decorations stand by themselves. Moreover, we know nothing yet of the depth of the decay between these waves.

(In the following chapter the diagram fig. 57, at end, may be useful for reference, though it is not described in detail till p. 118.)

CHAPTER V

RELATIONS OF DIFFERENT ACTIVITIES

(21) SUBJECTS IN VIIITH PERIOD

SO far we have only looked at Sculpture, as
being the most fully represented, and most
readily valued, product of civilisation. But it
must not be thought that it is the most essential product, or that other activities have necessarily the same phase of wave as we find in
sculpture. Most of the other evidences of
civilisation appear later than that of sculpture,
and our object in this chapter is to estimate the
order in which they are evolved and their rela-
tion one to another. We begin naturally with
the best-known period, that of the last six
centuries, and examine the changes in that
before looking to earlier periods. The great and
important elements of moral ideas and religion
are omitted here because they are so largely
subjective, and their standards necessarily vary
with the requirements of the phase of the
civilisation.

Sculpture and Architecture go closely together in all ages, so far as we can see. In
sculpture the turning point of freedom has been
here set at A.D. 1240, mainly on the strength

DIFFERENT ACTIVITIES

of the well-dated Bamberg sculptures, which are remote from Mediterranean tradition. In architecture, Salisbury Cathedral stands for the perfect acquirement of freedom and grace without the least trace of over-elaboration. As it was founded in 1220, and completed (without the steeple) before the consecration in 1258, this coincides as closely as possible with the highest point of sculpture. We are here following the test period of the disappearance of archaism, apart from the personal question of appreciation of style.

The next development is that of painting. Some of the drawings by Matthew of Paris, about 1240, are very beautiful, such as the royal marriage (MS. Cott. Nero, D.i), but yet not free of archaism. There is no work of Giotto that is beyond the archaic stage, down to 1330. The chapel of S. Felice at Padua shows that as early as 1379 complete freedom was attained by Altichiero and Jacopo d'Avanzo ; they were the earliest masters to stand clear of archaism, which was not fully passed by other men till about 1450. We may say, then, that the turning point in painting is 150 or 200 years later than that in sculpture.

In Literature we must compare only plain prose, as poetry and plays have by their nature an artificial structure. Bacon and Ben Jonson are at the turning point. Bacon, with his high education, retained the archaic structure ; while Jonson shows that in popular use archaism had gone, and many of his sentences might have been written at any later date ; 1600 may then be taken as the turning point of freedom in writing, and none can deny that it was the greatest age of vigour in literature.

In Music the development is so much nearer to our own time that it is difficult to estimate it impartially. Perhaps we may say that Haydn was still archaic in most of his life, but steps freely for the first time in his great symphonies of 1790 ; while Beethoven only shows some memories of archaism rarely in his earlier symphonies, from 1796 onward. Hence, perhaps, 1790 may be accepted as the turning point.

Our difficulty of estimation is still greater in later developments. In Mechanics, or the adaptation of long familiar principles and materials, the full freedom of design was certainly not attained in the earlier railway work. Brunel's tubular bridge, though new, was by no means a perfect adaptation to its requirements. Perhaps Baker's Forth Bridge may be the typical example of freedom from needless restriction, in meeting one of the oldest needs of man with methods and material already well known, apart from fresh discovery. Or it may be that further work will show that archaism has even clung to that. For the present we may put down 1890 as the close of archaism in mechanics.

It is obvious that in Natural Science discovery is still flowing rapidly, and that our conceptions have by no means outgrown the stage of casting off previous ideas, and only developing what is in hand. Material wealth is also still rapidly on the increase.

We can now summarise the turning points of the freedom from archaism in the VIIIth period as being at—

A.D. 1240 in Sculpture.
,, 1400 ,, Painting.
,, 1600 ,, Literature.
,, 1790 ,, Music.
,, 1890 ,, Mechanics.
after ,, 1910 ,, Science.
,, 1910 ,, Wealth.

(22) SUBJECTS IN VIITH PERIOD

The estimation of the dates of these several phases in the previous civilisation of the classical period is next in our view.

The Sculpture we have already estimated, as reaching the turning point at 450 B.C. Painting was of later development, but in the absence of any dated paintings of pre-Roman times, we can only glean a view from the vague descriptions and remarks preserved to us. Polygnotos (460 B.C.), whose style was strictly ethic, seems to have been almost parallel to Giotto in design. The establishment of light and shade and abandonment of flat tints is attributed to Apollodoros (400 B.C.); Zeuxis, by 400 B.C., scarcely adopted correct proportion. By about 350 Parrhasios, and Eupompos with his direct appeal to Nature, seem to have finally left archaism. Apelles appears to have belonged to the later full-blown age, the Raphael of his period. In Italy there is flat tint painting of high quality from Paestum, probably before 400 B.C., for soon after this date the Greeks were conquered by the Lucanians. The more advanced paintings of Vulci and Corneto cannot be dated by history. But there is nothing on this side discordant with the development in Greece. We may take, then, 350 B.C. as the turning point of archaism in painting.

In Literature the close of the archaic style, and development of complete freedom of structure and adaptation of the sentence, might perhaps be put between Thucydides and Xenophon, say at 380 B.C. in Greece. In Italy, on the contrary, it was later, and can hardly be put before Cicero (50 B.C.); we may adopt the mean date of 200 B.C.

In Music our knowledge is almost entirely of its theory, and not of its history of development in practice, so it is useless to try to judge its evolution from archaism.

DIFFERENT ACTIVITIES

The Mechanics of the Greeks continued without a break into Roman use. Demetrios Poliorketes (300 B.C.) greatly developed machines for siege purposes (*Diod.* XX, V). His great siege-tower was 150 feet high ; but such a structure does not demand as much resource and ability as the erection of obelisks. Those which Augustus erected were 78 and 71 feet high ; that of Caligula, 83 feet ; and that of Constantius, 105 feet. To set up such masses seems to prove a greater amount of mechanical facility and structure than is shown by any other Roman work. This skill was continued into the Lower Empire, as seen by the obelisk at Constantinople. In construction the greatest dome (that of the Pantheon), 140 feet across, dates probably from A.D. 120. The basilica of Maxentius (A.D. 310) is only 85 feet across the nave, and, vast as the whole is, it can hardly rank as a bolder work than the Pantheon. The date of full mechanical freedom may thus perhaps be put at the beginning of the first century, with a continuance scarcely abated till the IVth century.

Science, both mathematical and organic, continued to develop into Roman times. Strabo's "Introduction to Geography" (A.D. 20) is excellent in its geometry and its scientific spirit. But Ptolemy (A.D. 150), as a geometer and theoretical astronomer, and as a vast organizer of material in geography, gave the final freedom to these sciences. The enormous works of Galen (A.D. 180) did much the same for medical science. It seems doubtful if there was any advance in knowledge after A.D. 200, and, within one or two centuries later, ground was certainly being lost. We may take A.D. 150 as the point of freedom of thought from archaic hypothesis.

In observing Wealth we must either select the maximum of precious metals, or the maximum of invested capital of conveniences of life. Though our facts are very scanty, and our result must be more a general impression than a defined statement, yet the two stages must be kept apart. Alexander plundered the accumulated treasures of the Eastern world in Persia, and Rome gradually stripped the Greek world of all its wealth by conquest and taxation, as well as drawing largely from Gaul and Spain. Probably the 1st or 2nd century A.D. saw the greatest accumulation of gold. Certainly after Aurelius (A.D. 170) there is a sudden drop in the weight of the aureus, and there was no reign with a free coinage of gold except Severus Alexander. This points to the capital stock having been mainly exhausted by A.D. 170. probably by the prodigious waste in gilding during the first two centuries. The drain of buying off the barbarians came later. The

DIFFERENT ACTIVITIES

maximum of precious metals might, then, be set somewhere in the 1st century, say A.D. 50, before the gigantic waste of Nero's Golden House. The accumulated capital of the means and conveniences of life probably continued to grow till the beginning of the break-up, about A.D. 200. But in the less disturbed provinces, such as Britain, Egypt, and Syria, we can see the most widespread prosperity later, about A.D. 300, as shown by the principal abundance of buildings and settlements of that age.

The turning points of the civilisation of the VIIth period may, then, be stated as follows :—

> B.C. 450 in Sculpture.
> ,, 350 ,, Painting.
> ,, 200 ,, Literature.
> ,, 0 ,, Mechanics.
> A.D 150 ,, Science.
> ,, 200 ,, Wealth.

(23) SUBJECTS IN THE VITH PERIOD

Of the VIth period we can only judge in detail from Egypt, as the distinctions of succession in Greece are too slightly known in the Mykenaean age.

Sculpture, as we have noticed, passed from its last trace of archaism about 1550 B.C., early in the reign of Amenhotep I. Painting was fully free and natural by 1470, under Tahutmes III.

Of Literature there are few dateable remains. Akhenaten's great Hymn to the Aten seems fully developed in its structure and noble use of language in 1380 ; while the poem of Pentaur in 1290 is turgid. In the tales, the Taking of Joppa (1470 B.C.) is but an artless folk-tale. The Doomed Prince (about 1300 B.C.) is well composed. Anpu and Bata is as fully developed as any writing of this period, and can hardly be later than 1200 B.C. Perhaps 1350 B.C. may be taken as the date of the first freedom in style.

In Mechanics the largest masses, cut and erected, were the colossi of Ramessu II, at Thebes and at Tanis, of 1000 and 900 tons ; these were made about 1280 B.C.

Of Science we have no detailed accounts. The Wealth shown by the diffused comforts of life seems to have grown, down to Ramessu III, 1180, and magnificent objects are shown in the tomb of Aimadua, about 1140 B.C. There certainly was a decline after this.

The summary, then, stands for the VIth period as :—

B.C. 1550	in	Sculpture.
,, 1470 ?	,,	Painting.
,, 1350 ?	,,	Literature.
,, 1280	,,	Mechanics.
,, 1180	,,	Wealth.

DIFFERENT ACTIVITIES

For the Vth period our data are still more scanty. The sculpture freed itself at the rise of the XIIth dynasty (3450 B.C.). Painting was certainly free in the figures of the wrestlers at Beni Hasan, late in the reign of Senusert I, the burial being in his 43rd year (3396 B.C.).

Of Literature, the best example is the hymn to Senusert III, about 3320 B.C. ; and the Adventures of Sanehat were very probably written about this time, referring to persons of two or three generations earlier. Mechanically, the greatest work known is the cutting and placing of the quartzite monolithic tomb chamber of Amenemhat III (3270 B.C.).

Of Wealth we have little idea ; but it certainly increased down to the close of the dynasty about 3250 B.C., but probably not later.

The summary of the Vth period, then, is :—

> B.C. 3450 in Sculpture.
> ,, 3400 ,, Painting.
> ,, 3320 ,, Literature.
> ,, 3270 ,, Mechanics.
> ,, 3250 ,, Wealth.

REVOLUTIONS OF CIVILISATION

(25) Subjects in the IVth Period

In the IVth period—of the pyramid builders —the scanty data point to the following stages. Sculpture had emerged from the archaic by 4750 B.C., in the reign of Sneferu. Painting seems to have been a little later, as the geese of Nefermaat may be a generation after the tomb of Rahotep. The mechanical ability is difficult to distinguish from the purely architectural maximum. For accuracy on a large scale Khufu stands unapproached; but the flint paint-slab of Assa is the most highly finished piece of work of this period. We know so little of the history of literature or wealth in this period that we cannot hope to estimate their exact position.

The summary of the IVth period is thus :—

> B.C. 4750 in Sculpture.
> ,, 4700 ? ,, Painting.
> ,, 4650 ? ,, Mechanics.

In these last three periods it may well be said that we are trusting to only one or two examples of some subjects that happen to have survived. But it must be remembered that it is the work of the fullest age that is most likely to survive, and it is the literature of the principal age that is the most valued and copied.

We may now review all the stages of civilisation together, taking the earliest phase, that of sculpture, as the zero of each period.

	VIII.	VII.	VI.	V.	IV.
Zero.	1240 A.D.	450 B.C.	1550 B.C.	3450 B.C.	4750 B.C.
Sculpture	0	0	0	0	0
Painting	160	100	80	50	50?
Literature	360	200	200	130	—
Mechanics	550	450	270	180	100?
Science	650 +	600	—	—	—
Wealth	650 +	650	370	200	—

Thus the order of development of the successive phases of each period is usually the same, though the intervals lengthened in the later ages.

CHAPTER VI

THE NATIONAL VIEW OF CIVILISATION

(26) THE HIGHEST AND LOWEST CONDITIONS

THE comparison of the successive periods may usefully be made by defining the greatest feature of each period in Egypt or Europe, and the nature of the collapse at the close of each period in Europe by conquest.

GREATEST FEATURE.	COLLAPSE IN EUROPE.
IV. Power of construction (IV dynasty).	
	Extermination of the conquered (?).
V. Foreign connections (XII dynasty).	
	Destruction of ma'es only (?).
VI. Utilising of natural products (XVIII dynasty).	
	Slavery (Dorians).
VII. Cataloguing of Nature (Roman).	
	Taking share of property (North races).
VIII. Utilising natural forces (Modern).	

We can thus see the widening of the outlook in the summer of each period, and the amelioration of the collapse in the winter. This is the real nature of human progress.

NATIONAL VIEW OF CIVILISATION

So far we have only regarded the Mediterranean and European civilisation, which has the same phase throughout: But that is not necessarily the phase in other parts of the world. In the Euphrates and Tigris system there was always a strong civilisation, which seems to have begun in the highlands to the east of the great valley. The mound of Susa accumulated 26 feet in 4000 years, and if the 50 feet of ruin below that grew at the same rate that would imply a beginning in 12,000 B.C. If it only grew at the rate found in Palestine mounds, then it dates from 6000 B.C. Probably we have to deal with a culture as early as any traced in Egypt.

We cannot here distinguish the phase as exactly as we can on the Mediterranean, and we must merely state the most notable rulers, from the artistic point of view, in each period.

	B.C.	YEARS.
Enneatum	4450 (?)	
		—700 (?)
Naramsin	3750	
		—1650
Khammurabi	2100	
		—1460
Ashurbanipal	640	
		—1460
El Mamun A.D.	820	

REVOLUTIONS OF CIVILISATION

The first of these periods is quite uncertain, as there is nothing to show whether such a stage was not attained earlier. The average of the three defined periods is 1520 years, which is not far from the 1320 years' average on the Mediterranean. The time by which the Eastern period anticipates the Western is :—

EAST.		WEST.		DIFFERENCE.
B.C. 3750	..	3450	..	300
,, 2100	..	1550	..	550
,, 640	..	450	..	190
A.D. 820	..	1240	..	420
			Average	365

Thus the Eastern phase, on the whole, keeps about 3½ centuries in advance of the Mediterranean, varying from 2 to 5½ centuries.

These results give some insight into the general meaning of historical conditions. The impression that civilisation always comes from the East is due to the East being a few centuries ahead of the West in its phase. Thus on the rise of a wave the East is more civilised ; while on the fall of a wave—which does not attract attention—it is less civilised.

The cause of the constant struggle between East and West is likewise seen to be due to the difference of phases. If Mesopotamia and Europe were in the same phase, there would be a balance of power, as there is around the Mediterranean, when even a political ascendancy does not involve a change of population. But with Mesopotamia always leading, it is bound, politically, to overrun the West a few centuries before the rise of the West in each period. The Mediterranean was almost an Arab lake at the time of El Mamun ; Persia dominated all the civilised Mediterranean in the sixth century B.C. Yet, on the whole, the West more usually controls the East, because from the time of its maximum, during the gradual decline of each period, it is always on a higher plane than the East.

In some other cases also the period from one wave of greatness to the next can be traced. In India, Asoka had the greatest power known in ancient times, including all India (except the southern tip), Kashmir, Afghanistan, and Beluchistan. This rule was at its height in 250 B.C. The next great age of rule was on the completion of the Mogul Empire (A.D. 1550). The interval is 1800 years.

In Mexico, the highly civilised Maya kingdom is traditionally stated to have been founded in the Xth century B.C. On its fall, it was succeeded by the Toltecs, also highly civilised, in the VIth century A.D. The interval is 1500 years.

Thus the period of a civilisation is :—

	PERIOD.
Mediterranean, average	1330 years.
(or, omitting the earliest,	1500)
Mesopotamia, average	1520 ,,
India, one period	1800 ,,
Mexico ,, about	1500 ,,

It is evident, therefore, that the length of period is practically alike in different parts of the globe, suggesting that it is due to the human constitution rather than to external causes. The phase, however, varies greatly.

(28) THE PHASE BELONGING TO FOLK, NOT TO LAND

Here another enquiry must be made : Does this phase in each place belong to the country or to the people ? The only way we can study this is by seeing examples where a whole people have migrated and expelled a race which had a different phase. Does their subsequent history agree with their own old phase, or with that of their new country ? We cannot take any modern movements, as we cannot yet see what may be the phase of the immigrants' civilisation ; and in early times we do not know enough of the sources or nature of immigrations before the classical period. The large northern movements are out of count, as the northmen seem (by their exquisite early bronze work) to have had the same phase as the rest of Europe.

The few movements which we can examine are those of the Etruscans (if an Asiatic people), the Greeks in Bactria, and the Arabs in Spain. The most curious feature of the Roman history is the disappearance of the civilisation of Etruria. The Etrurian sages themselves put their period as 1100 years, ending at 88 B.C., in the passage which we have quoted in the beginning. Their great civilisation, shown by engineering works, great fortress cities, and richly painted tombs, all vanishes before the Imperial period. When Rome was greatest and Italy was most secure, and had the fullest opportunities for development, Etruria is absolutely a blank page. Cisalpine Gaul—the plain of Lombardy—had some political importance and produced some important men ; but not so Etruria. We must see that the Etruscan civilisation was in a phase that was some centuries before that of Greece and Rome. The source of the Etruscans has been endlessly debated ; but they certainly were foreign to Italy, and as foreigners they brought with them a phase of civilisation which was not that of the Mediterranean or of Western Europe.

Of the Greeks in Bactria we know little. But certainly for some three or four centuries they show a civilisation which was higher than

the native. Now the East was highly civilised ;
Persia was far more advanced than Greece at
500 B.C., and probably at 400. For the Greek,
therefore, to retain a superiority to the Eastern
implies that he kept his own phase, which was
two or three centuries later.

The Arabs in Spain are strangely neglected
in current histories. To write of mediaeval
Europe without them is to ignore the principal
civilisation of the period. The fullest histories,
the strongest literature, the largest life, were all
south of the Pyrenees throughout the Dark
Ages. Yet this civilisation occupies five lines
out of five hundred pages in the best-known
handbook on that period. We read, in the Arab
historians, of different kings having elaborate
gardens with every variety of plant ; of the
literary academy to whom new poems were re-
cited ; of the fund for the endowment of learned
men, and the attraction of scholars from all
parts of the world. The crowning glory was
the library of Al Hakem, who in 970 A.D. entirely filled a palace at Cordova with books
sought from the whole known world. The
classified shelves of this library held 600,000
volumes, all catalogued and in order. The
political power was rather earlier, as its greatest
extent was when Abd er Rahman reached the
middle of France in 732. When we look further,
we see that by 1030 they deplore the rapid

deterioration of the people ; and by 1144 a democratic system began, setting up and over-throwing rulers with great frequency by the power of the *vox populi*. This regular feature of a decaying civilisation shows that it had certainly passed all its stages of growth and glory. These dates of political power, literature, and decay entirely conform to the Mesopotamian phase, and are contrary to the European phase.

Thus, apparently in the case of the Etruscan in Italy and of the Greek in the East, and certainly among the Arabs in Spain, it is seen that the phase of an intrusive people is that of their source, and not that of their new region. The phase of civilisation is inherent in the people, and is not due to the circumstances of their position.

When the phase of each group of civilisation has been further defined, it may be possible to use the phase of civilisation as a criterion of the source of an invading people. The instance already noted of the Etruscan phase, illustrates this ; their greatest power was about 600 B.C., which was that of the phase of Mesopotamian civilisation. Possibly the phase clings to a race for ages ; certainly the most flourishing period of mediaeval Tuscany was earlier than that of the rest of Italy by a few centuries, just as it had been earlier in the classical times.

In connection with this, it may be noted how the conquest and settlement of each country of Europe by Rome is reflected in its later history. The order of Roman influence was Italy, Spain, France, England, Germany ; and this is the order of political power of these countries in the last few centuries.

(29) The Breaks between Periods

The next question is that of the separation of one period from another. We have represented the wave of civilisation as falling to a *minimum*, and then suddenly rising again. To what is this change due ? In every case in which we can examine the history sufficiently, we find that there was a fresh race coming into the country when the wave was at its lowest. In short, every civilisation of a settled population tends to incessant decay from its *maximum* condition ; and this decay continues until it is too weak to initiate anything, when a fresh race comes in, and utilises the old stock to graft on, both in blood and culture. As soon as the mixture is well started, it rapidly grows on the old soil, and produces a new wave of civilisation. There is no new generation without a mixture of blood, parthenogenesis is unknown in the birth of nations. Further on we shall deal with some of the natural results of this condition.

We will now review the breaks between the periods in Europe and in Egypt, to show the reasons for the broad statement just made. The movements of peoples always extend over some centuries, and we can only adopt the dates at which the actual race-mixture seems to have occurred.

The break between the classical and mediaeval periods, VII and VIII, is the most familiar. It is needless to detail here the continuous flow of migrations from the north of Europe to the south, and from the Asiatic side westwards ; between A.D. 300 and 600, fifteen different races broke bounds, belonging to half a dozen different stocks (see *Migrations*, Huxley lecture, 1906). We here take 450 A.D. as the main date of mixture, though much was going on for two centuries before that, and also after it.

The beginning of the classical period (VII), and the close of the Mykenaean (VI), has been partly understood from recent discoveries. The old tradition of the " Return of the Herakleidai," is placed about 1200 B.C. The Cretan civilisation is supposed to have been swamped during the alliance wars on Egypt, 1194 B.C. The Egyptian connections with Greece by dated objects all cease at this date. Hence 1200 B.C. may be taken as the date of the main change.

The breaks from the Middle Cretan (V) to the Late Cretan or Mykenaean (VI), and from the Early Cretan (IV) to the Middle Cretan (V), were at approximately the dates of the breaks in Egypt, but cannot be otherwise dated from Greek sources.

In Egypt the change from period VII to VIII, is particularly definitely fixed by the Arab invasion in 641 A.D. After the main body other tribes of Arabs came in, down to the ninth century; on the other hand there had been a filtering before the great migration, as Arab horsemen were Roman auxiliaries in Egypt many centuries earlier.

The break of the VIth period is not well defined in Egypt, but was made up of various immigrations, starting the VIIth period with Easterners, 950 B.C., Ethiopians, 750 B.C., and Libyans from then onward.

The VIth period was brought in by the Hyksos migration, 2600 B.C. There had been a filtering in of Eastern people before, and two Mesopotamians even became kings of Egypt; also there was probably a constant flow of further immigrants, as exemplified by Terah and Abram, about four or five hundred years later. Probably we might date the mixture of Hyksos as beginning about 2600 B.C.

The Vth period is indicated by the collapse of Egyptian work after the VIth dynasty; and the appearance, at the close of the VIth dynasty and onwards, of foreign button-seals, which are connected with the Cretan products, 4000 B.C.

The IVth period, of the pyramid builders, apparently began with the IIIrd dynasty. There is continuous decline in work down to the close of the IInd dynasty, and early in the IIIrd; yet by the end of the IIIrd dynasty there had arisen the finest Egyptian art. The break indicated by the change of dynasty is doubtless the coming in of the new period. This is dated to 5000 B.C.

The rise of the IIIrd period is lost in the darkness of the predynastic age. The highest point of the sculptor we have shown (by the hawks) to belong to Zer, 5400 B.C. Before that there was 150 years to the beginning of the Ist dynasty, and 350 years of kings before that (dynasty O), making 500 years recorded before the age of the best sculpture. But this is only the time of a settled rule, and the duration of the confusion of the conquest has to be added, perhaps a century more.

The invasion dates, when a new period of civilisation is started, may be compared with the sculpture phases thus :—

PERIOD.	INVASION.	GROWTH.	SCULPTURE.
III ..	6000 ? ..	600 ? ..	5400 B.C.
IV ..	4960 ..	150 ..	4750
V ..	4000 ..	550 ..	3450
VI ..	2600 ..	1050 ..	1550
VII ..	1200 ..	750 ..	450
VIII ..	450 ..	800 ..	1240 A.D.

REVOLUTIONS OF CIVILISATION

It is obvious that the pyramid builders came in upon the early dynastic people abnormally soon ; taking only 150 years to rise to a fresh maximum. We know so little of the historical conditions, that we cannot see the meaning of this. Perhaps it should be rather regarded as a double maximum of one period, divided in the same way as the classical age was parted into a Greek and a Roman maximum.

(30) The Diagram of Periods

We are now in a position to review all the dates for the various phases of each period in a combined diagram (see fig. 57 at end). Each period is shown by a line sloping down toward the right hand. The scale of the period runs along the line, as marked in the bottom period, and the line slopes down according to the vertical scale ruled in millennia. Thus each line of a period ends at the same level as the next period line begins. These period lines may be looked on as a continuous spiral around a cylinder, divided at each invasion. The purpose of thus arranging the facts is to enable all of the periods to be readily compared in their main features. There is no absolute fixing of the successive lines of periods one below the other. Many different adjustments might be made, and one must be arbitrarily

selected. The rise or close of each period
(the ends of the period-lines) are not satis-
factory, for a period may come to an abrupt
break, as did the VIth. None of the phases
of a period are so well defined as the close of
archaism, and attainment of complete freedom,
in sculpture. The later the period the more
the various phases diverge, and it is not well
to place the earliest of the phases in a vertical
column, as the other phases will spread so
far to the right in later periods. The fairest
arrangement for comparison seems to be
to take the best-defined phase—the sculpture—
as the connecting link, and to set the sculpture
phases one below the other in a line square
with the slope of the period lines. The earlier
periods are necessarily based upon the Egyptian
examples, and the later periods upon the
European examples, as being the best-defined
in each case. So much for the construction
of the diagram.

Now we turn to reading the diagram, and
drawing conclusions from it. The first striking
feature is the much wider spread of the phases
as the periods descend. This means that
there are lesser intervals of barbarism between
the civilisations, and that the civilisation
phase in each period is longer at each recurrence. This is in accord with the common
idea that the world is getting more civilised

as the ages go on, in spite of the crushing fact that in many kinds of civilisation the successive recurrences show no improvement. Egyptian construction is as good in the IVth period as anything done in the four later periods. Art is as good in the IVth or VIth or VIIth as it has ever been later, though differing in its nature. Thus, while the best work in art is no better in successive periods, the total amount of civilisation is greater, because it is longer. The gain is in quantity and not quality.

Another result of this widening out of the phases is to separate the best period of each form of culture. Thus in the early days the arts of sculpture and painting, mechanics, and wealth, were all nearly contemporaneous. Hence there was artistic mechanics, executed by wealth. But as the phases space out further, the art is decadent before the mechanical ability is free, and before the wealth has grown. Hence the increasingly tasteless use of wealth by the late Mykenaean, the Roman, or the modern man. A strange feature of these successive periods is the sudden raid of northerners, that breaks through to the south of Europe in the midst of the most flourishing age, and leaves no permanent trace. In 1527 A.D. the raid on Rome and its horrible sacking by the Germans under the

NATIONAL VIEW OF CIVILISATION

Constable de Bourbon (see "Germans" on diagram) was the greatest blow the city received since Totila. As Gibbon says, "the ravages of the Barbarians, whom Alaric had led from the banks of the Danube, were less destructive than the hostilities exercised by the troops of Charles the Fifth." In 390 B.C. the Kelts laid Rome waste with fire and sword, and in 279 they largely plundered Greece (see "Kelts" in diagram). In the "Late Minoan II" period, or 1500 B.C., was the great catastrophe of the destruction of the Palace of Knossos, apparently by barbarians, who, nevertheless, did not interrupt the general culture. The "Middle Minoan II" period, about the XIIth Egyptian dynasty, or 3300 B.C., is cut short by a general catastrophe, which does not hinder the immediate resumption of the civilisation by building the second palace (Evans, *Essai de Classification*). Thus in four successive periods—that is, so far back as our detailed knowledge extends—we see that southern Europe at its brightest has been suddenly clouded by a northern storm which has left no permanent change.

The principal conqueror of each period has arisen at the same phase. In period VIII Napoleon is marked with N below the line, between Literature and Mechanics. In period VII Caesar, marked C, is in the same position.

In period VI Ramessu II (R) comes at L & M, in the same connection. In period V Senusert III (S), the main Egyptian conqueror in that period, coincides with L.

With regard to the beginning and end of each period, the exact assignment is difficult, as the mixture of the incoming race is usually gradual, extending over a century or more. Hence it is not surprising if we have a couple of centuries' variation in the period of growth before the phase of sculpture. The rather longer interval between the Vth and VIth civilisations is seen to be due to the slower development of the VIth, the Vth ending normally. On the other hand, the short interval between the VIth and VIIth is seen to be due to the violent end of the VIth, cutting off entirely the normal four centuries, or so, of slow decay after the maximum of wealth was attained. Thus the study of the diagram shows clearly what were the exact seats of the irregularities of the periods.

(31) STAGES OF GOVERNMENT

Forms of government are left to the last, as the regulation of daily affairs, and the repression of wrong, is of little meaning in civilisation, when compared with the great formative interests of man's mind, whose phases we have studied. It is true that man thinks and talks much about government, in all ages. But then the concern of man is no measure of the real value of a subject, as appears by his perennial interest in gambling, which now occupies a large part of the printing in this country. So also government is of great concern, but of little import. Constitutional History is a barren figment compared with the permanent value of Art, Literature, Science, or Economics. What man *does* is the essential in each civilisation, how he advances in capacities, and what he bequeaths to future ages ; the relations between the different classes of a country are merely subsidiary. England, France, and Russia will be remembered by Newton, Pasteur, and Mendelieff, when all their forms of government are forgotten.

At every invasion by a new people, which, as we have seen, is the necessary foundation of a new period of civilisation, there must be strong personal rule. The holding together of the invaders, the decisive subjection of the invaded, the strife of the fusion of peoples, all require an autocracy of greater or less scope. This period lasts during four to six centuries.

The next stage is an oligarchy, when leadership is still essential, but the unity of the country can be maintained by law instead of by autocracy. This stage varies in length ; in Greece and Rome it was about four centuries, in Mediaeval Europe about five or six centuries.

Then gradually the transformation to a democracy takes place ; beginning about the great phase of literature in Greece, Rome, and Modern Europe. During this time—of about four centuries—wealth—that is, the accumulated capital of facilities—continues to increase. When democracy has attained full power, the majority without capital necessarily eat up the capital of the minority, and the civilisation steadily decays, until the inferior population is swept away to make room for a fitter people. The consumption of all the resources of the Roman empire, from the second century when democracy was dominant, until the Gothic kingdom arose on its ruin, is the best-known example in detail. Such is the regular connection of .the forms of government, or the relations of classes, which is inherent in the conditions of the revolutions of civilisation.

CHAPTER VII

CONDITIONS OF CIVILISATION

(32) ADVANCE THROUGH STRIFE

IN another point of view the periods of civilisation bear a fresh meaning. There is no advance without strife. Man must strive with Nature or with man, if he is not to fall back and degenerate. The harder a nation strives, the more capable it will be. This is not only the slow result of selection, but it is the immediate result in each individual, produced by the attitude of his mind. The Northern nations, accustomed to striving against climate, thrive vastly when they get into easier countries, until their tone is let down to their conditions. Hence almost all migration is from colder to warmer climates. And within the same country—as in England at present—there is a steady flow of families pushing south.

This necessity of striving implies a rapid advance during the centuries after an invasion. There is the whole organization of the new period to be evolved by continual strife of ideas and personalities, there is the new civilisation to be evolved by striving of ideals until a definite platform is reached. So soon as each subject loses its archaism and reaches full freedom of expression, there is no more strife with difficulties and uncertainties of mode ; then, strife being ended, decay sets in shortly after.

Further the accumulation of the facilities of life, or capital in every form, diminishes the need for striving. There is so much the less worth striving for, there is so much more to enjoy without strife. Hence, the easier life is rendered, the more easy is decay and degradation. The maximum of wealth must inevitably lead to the downfall.

(33) Causes of Period

We have now seen how general is the regular recurrence of civilisation in all countries that we have examined, and how constant is the order of its phases. Another question remains to us, Why is this period so far regular ? What determines the spring, summer, and autumn of the Great Year ?

The first and most obvious cause would be periodical changes of climate. The American expedition to Turkestan has brought to light regular cycles of wet and dry climate there ; and Mr. Huntington has pointed out the effects of such cycles of climate in Western Asia and Greece (*R. Geog. Soc.*, 26 May, 1910). It is clear that such changes have an effect in precipitating upon the richer lands the pastoral races, who live on lands too dry for agriculture. We find an age of famines along with such movements, and continuing after them. The Hyksos movement from the Arabian plains was followed by famine in Syria, and then seven years' famine in Egypt. The Arab movement started from a great famine in A.D. 600, followed by famines during four centuries, in 866, 873, 928, 929, 969, 970, 1025, 1055, 1065, yearly, to 1072, and then some sporadic famines in 1201, 1264, 1295. These were caused by the low Nile in Egypt, which implies a short supply in Abyssinia. Thus the increased dryness does accompany an age of migration, and may be one cause for it.

But that will not account for the regular phases already described. Nor can it account for a race keeping to its own phase, when it has passed into a country of a different phase, as we have noticed.

There may be a normal rate of change from stage to stage, produced by the process of the human mind. Each generation may average a certain extent of change, as each year averages a certain amount of growth or decay in the body. Yet against this as an entire·cause there is the alteration in the closeness of the phases; the different activities were grouped much more closely together in early times, they are by now separated by some generations each. This may imply that each subject is more elaborately developed as it comes forward, and absorbs all the best intellect for a longer time, and so postpones the rise of the next subject.

There is, however, another possible cause of the length of period. The rise of the new civilisation is conditioned by an immigration of a different people. That is to say, it arises from a mixture of two different stocks. That effect of mixture cannot take place all at once. There are barriers of antipathy, barriers of creed, barriers of social standing, but every barrier to race-fusion gives way in time, when two races are in contact. Even if every marriage in the first generation was a mixed one, that would only give two elements of the needful fusion to each child; and what seems to be needed is an ancestry of all the elements of two different races completely intermingled to produce a new era of activities. Now, if generations average 30 years, we may take it that each man has 10 ancestors a century ago, apart from related marriages. Hence each man has a million ancestors in six centuries,

10 millions in seven centuries, 100 millions in eight centuries. Thus (apart from related marriages) seven or eight centuries of mixture of two races ensures that, in any ordinary-sized country, the full maximum number of different ancestors are blended, and every strain of one race has crossed with every strain of the other. This is the period of greatest ability, beginning about eight centuries after the mixture, and lasting for four or five centuries in different subjects. The extension of the time may well balance the delay in mixture due to related marriages. Thus we may say that the complete crossing of two races produces the maximum of ability, and that, from that point, repeated generations diminish the ability. This may well be the basal cause of the· length of period which we have noticed, as it well accords with it in the time required. But probably each of the other causes before noted may bear a part. For instance, a dry period and famine may precipitate a migration which cuts short a civilisation, as in period VI.

(34) THE FUTURE

And what of the Future ? We have at last a fairly consistent view of the whole system of civilisation, its causes of development, its stages of growth and decay. How far can that suggest the future ? This is by no means a fatalist view ; for there is as much difference between an unhealthy and a healthy civilisation—as much to care for and strive for—as there is between a man worn out by middle life and one who is vigorous and useful to a green old age.

If we look at the diagram of all the stages (fig. 57) we see that the widening apart of the stages means that wealth of improvements can be accumulated later in each stage, and the maximum of wealth in Europe promises in our own stage to reach to near the end of our period, when an entire mixture with another race will be requisite. We do not see any tendency to shorten the stage of growth in the successive periods ; that may be because it is conditioned by complete crossing of the two stocks, as we have noticed. So that the production of a new European art, and its subsequent activities, cannot be expected for many centuries.

But are not the conditions of the world so radically altered that no past phenomena will be repeated again ? The mixture of race going on in many countries at present will tend to fuse the whole world, owing to the ease of communication which has never existed before. In a few centuries will not the people of every country be blended, and be alike ? Hardly so, as the conditions of climate will always make men black or white ; the conditions of the countries will always separate pastoral, agricultural, and manufacturing communities. The present rate of spread is the effect of a sudden facility. It will tend to diminish, as suitable conditions are found and established ; and a more stable adjustment of population will arise in future. It is parallel to the great diffusion which must have taken place on the development of shipping.

Yet if the view becomes really grasped, that the source of every civilisation has lain in race mixture, it may be that eugenics will, in some future civilisation, carefully segregate fine races, and prohibit continual mixture, until they have a distinct type, which will start a new civilisation when transplanted. The future progress of man may depend as much on isolation to establish a type, as on fusion of types when established.

INDEX

133

INDEX

WILLIAM BRENDON AND SON, LTD. PRINTERS, PLYMOUTH

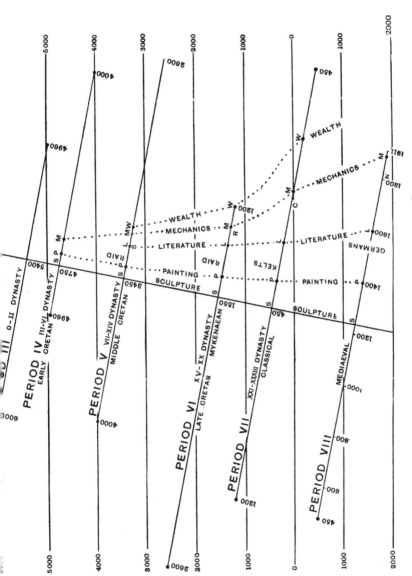

57. THE PERIODS AND PHASES OF MEDITERRANEAN CIVILISATION.

To be placed at end of Vol.

www.ingramcontent.com/pod-product-compliance
Ingram Content Group UK Ltd.
Pitfield, Milton Keynes, MK11 3LW, UK
UKHW042151280225
455719UK00001B/261